A Bum Deal: Exploring Feelings with Felines

Written by Tammy MacKenzie BSc RPN, Olya Vespyansky LPN, and Ben Mikkelsen

Illustrated by Olya Vespyansky and Ben Mikkelsen. Two of the coolest cats around.

Copyright © (2023) by Tammy Mackenzie BSc RPN, Olya Vespyansky LPN, Ben Mikkelsen all right reserved.

ISBN e-book: 9781738750702

ISBN print: 9798378207152

Published by Tammy MacKenzie BSc RPN

Without limiting the rights under copyright reserved above, no part of this publication may be reproduced, stored in, or introduced

into a database and retrieval system or transmitted in any form or by any means (electronic, mechanical, photocopying, recording or otherwise) without the prior written permission of the owner of copyright. No portion of this book may be reproduced in any form without written permission from the publisher or author, except as permitted by U.S. and Canada copyright law.

I gained the permission of the cat Moms and Dads to use the real names of their cats in these poems.

Dedication

We would like to dedicate this book to all those coping with a mental health issue.
Many of the best people are.
You are not alone.

We would also like to dedicate this book to our team of cats Java, Noodle, Willy, Ouija, Salem and Kyla. Without their inspiration, comfort, and healing, this book would not have been written.

With Gratiude

With deep gratitude and many head bunts of thanks to our Instagram followers of Catpoems50. You gave us the confidence to create this book.

Cat high fives to our Beta readers and other helpers to format this book including my husband, Jenny, Sue, and Grace. Ben thanks his wife, Joanna for her love and support during the process of creating this book.

Batting those strings of creative ideas around together and weaving this mental health mat to lay on or cuddle with, to cry over, and smile with (or laugh at, that's good too) has been deeply therapeutic.

Introduction

It's ok to shatter. Life can be like juggling a dozen raw eggs all at once. Many of us have, more than once. Sometimes life hands us a bum deal. People use different ways of putting themselves back together. Sometimes we try to glue ourselves back together with chocolate, but that melts and gets all over everything and isn't strong enough to hold. Alcohol is a choice, but that's a liquid, so it leaks and gets all over everything. Plus, it ultimately makes depression and anxiety worse over time.

The Japanese use gold and glue to hold together their precious porcelain, but that might make us too expensive; we'd get mugged. I'm still not immune to the occasional catastrophic thought. Stick with using gold on your teeth. I vote we choose therapy which gets us closer to our goal of being whole, slightly cracked perhaps, which really is more fun, but whole again. Let's give cat therapy a try.

I don't have a PhD in cats, but I am a Registered Psychiatric Nurse with a Bachelors degree in

Health Sciences and Dr. Purrs A. Lot's staff nurse. More than one patient has told me the only reason they chose not to kill themselves was because of the love and worry about what would happen to their beloved pet. I was surprised when I was first told this early in my nursing career. Life has given me the opportunity to understand how protective our pets can be for our health. I can vouch for the effectiveness of cat therapy due to my own experiences with it. I grew up with 2 cats, I have had three cats in my adult life all of whom I have loved obsessively, and am now fostering Olya's cats, whom I adore and have to keep reminding myself I need to give them back when she finds a new apartment that accepts pets. Olya, you can't have them, just kittening...

Collectively, our cats soften our lives. My cats helped me through grief at a time when I was experiencing an overwhelming amount of illness and worry in my life. My mother-in-law was sick, my mom was sick and my two wonderful children have chronic health conditions to cope with. As if that wasn't enough, I found myself on the front lines of COVID-19. I work on a Geriatric psychiatry unit, so we became very protective of our patients. COVID-19 snuck in the door anyway and we cared for those patients. It was scary in the beginning when we knew little about the illness. I lost my energy and appetite.

I increased my medication a little and took a few weeks off work. My cats, even pictures of cats and cat videos, calmed me significantly while waiting for my anti-depressant medication increase to work. They made me happy enough to eat again. Gradually my energy came back too. They were life affirming since the two strongest women I have ever known were dying due to dementia.

My good friend Olya, was living alone during the pandemic. She would talk to and cuddle her cats, which kept her sane. Her cats are very chatty, told her great stores and are great listeners. Ben, the other illustrator of this book and a good friend, told me that his cat helped his young son, who has autism, to self regulate his emotions for his cat brother.

We are all deeply grateful to our cats for their love and companionship. Let's put ourselves back together using cats, which of course, come with a lot of cat hair. Technically, does this mean we have to felt ourselves back together? I'm kittening...There are risks of course, such as sprouting cat hair between your toes, getting tickled on your nose, and there are the tiny scars of cat acupuncture on your skin as a side effect. Your couch might get them too.

The benefits of cat therapy far outweigh the risks. You will develop a fuzzy buffer against the world. both physically and emotionally. A lot of cat hair on your clothes provides extra insulation and texture. You will also feel an abundance of love in your life. Cats will bunt you into smiling and play with you while you laugh at their funny antics.

More laughter in life can heal. Mayo Clinic 2021, list a multitude of ways through which laughter heals and builds resilience. Humour releases chemicals in the brain (picture nano kittens) running around making new and positive connections. They give the best cuddles and body bunts, which bring comfort and joy...but not to Christmas trees... Cats purr at 25 to 150 hertz. Healing frequencies , similar to TENS devices used for treating pain. Be forewarned, it's hard to stop at just one cat therapist. If you need a team of them, we support you.

These poems are a collection of all the ways our cats have helped us catch those mice of loneliness, anxiety, depression and a plain old bad day. Cats allowed us to see hope when we thought there was none. Allowed us to have better and closer relationships with each other and ourselves. Some of these poems tackle serious issues, while others are just good fun. Your cat therapist will tell you to have more fun where you can find it, and here it is! Cat fur lets in the light and reflects it back to you like a cat hug when you need it most.

The health advice given in this book by the well known Cat Therapist, Dr. Purrs A. Lot, is not meant to replace that of your own doctor or therapist. This book contains QR codes you can scan to bring you to mental health web sites that you may find interesting and helpful. I certainly have used them over the years to keep me on track. Don't strive for purrrfection with your mental health. Do the best you can. Even one change can make all the difference. The end of this book contains a list of Online mental health resources with scan-able QR codes. Feel free to use them or not. Enjoy these poems from our hearts and minds to yours. We, and your cats stand with you in this mouse ridden world.

I used the gender neutral pronoun 'they' in some of the poems to help promote acceptance and inclusiveness.

DISCLAIMER: The authors if this book are not paid by the websites recommended in this book.

CONTACT ME: Tammy MacKenzie BSc RPN on Instagram catpoems50 or use Facebook messenger.

A Bum Deal: Exploring Feelings with Felines

1. Cat Therapy — 15
2. Dr. Purrs A. Lot — 16
3. Bum Deal — 17
4. Wake Up! — 18
5. Cat Physical Therapist — 19
6. Chilling — 20
7. Black Luck — 21
8. Queen of Cats — 22
9. Saws — 23
10. Roll Out the Mat! — 24
11. Cat Plant — 25
12. Cat Acupuncturist — 26
13. Saviour — 27
14. Fashionistia — 28

15.	Hold it!	29
16.	Love or Jealousy	30
17.	Gone!	31
18.	Cat's Magic	32
19.	Alone Time	33
20.	Cat Training	34
21.	Soft Predator	35
22.	Hat Chase	36
23.	Secret Keeper	37
24.	Sacrifice	38
25.	Feline Fling	39
26.	Cat Friendship	40
27.	Ear Gears	41
28.	Nine Lives	42
29.	Fishy	43
30.	Growing Up	44
31.	Cat Yoga	45
32.	Creative Play	46
33.	Walking Beans	47
34.	Amusement Park?	48

35.	Christmas Glitter	49
36.	Cat Love	50
37.	Sommelier Cat	51
38.	Cat Scam	52
39.	Cat Fever	53
40.	Cat Cure	54
41.	Miss You	55
42.	Mice Dreams	56
43.	Diva	57
44.	Black Pearls	58
45.	0200-0530	59
46.	Cat Help	60
47.	Sous Chef	61
48.	Night Watch	62
49.	Trouble!	63
50.	Bathtub Pub	64
51.	Live Mouse!	65
52.	Rad Cats	66
53.	Simply Heartfelt	67
54.	Play Time	68

55.	Insomnia	69
56.	Persistence	70
57.	Tutor	71
58.	Gifts	72
59.	Dad's Gone	73
60.	Spooky Chair	74
61.	Soft Claws	75
62.	Shadows	76
63.	Tight Rope Walker	77
64.	Be Furbulous	78
65.	Dish Duty	79
66.	Fussy Cat	80
67.	A Break in my Clouds	81
68.	Cat Rescue	82
69.	Feline Fantasy	83
70.	Invasion	84
71.	Cat Healing	85
72.	Comfort	86
73.	Cat Night Nurse	87
74.	Fishbowl Margarita	88

75.	Feline Frolicking	89
76.	Human Friend	90
77.	Cozy Time	91
78.	Christmas Elf	92
79.	Cat Nip	93
80.	Champagne Bubbles	94
81.	Cat Croissant	95
82.	Black Crystal	96
83.	Major Tom	97
	Online Mental Health Resources	100

Cat Therapy

When the world has crushed me and I have crumbled,
cats add a soft landing to my wcrld.
Cats make me laugh,
set me back on my path.
Cat therapy heals me when I have stumbled.

 Dr. Purrs A. Lot: Your cat is your pawson on your life's journey. They add more healing humour to life. Scan QR code for article.

Dr. Purrs A. Lot

Prescription:
Pet, play and cuddle with
your cat,
as needed (prn).
No maximum dose,
no side effects.
Takes effect immediately.

Bum Deal

My cat stands on my chest and stares,
down at my sleeping face and dares,
me to get up.
She shows me her rump!
So I fly from the bed towards the stairs!

Dr. Purrs A. Lot: Find what motivates you out of bed. A can of tuna with a sprinkle of catnip, perhaps? Just like mom used to make!

Wake Up!

Waiting for myself to wake up,
my two cats were determined to help.
One cat at a time,
they danced up my spine.
To face my day, I needed that help!

Dr. Purrs A. Lot: A cat will get you out of bed at the same time every morning and help you stick to your routine. Your cat alarm may go off early, snooze not included.

Cat Physical Therapist

Stiff neck and headache,
did I lay in bed too long, hiding from the world?
Pat, pat, "get up" says my cat therapist.
I grab the shoestring, I grab the mousy,
the exercise tools.
The exercises,
Lift right arm, throw mousy,

cat therapist chases mousy,
bend over, pick up mousy
Cat therapist demands I repeat,
until they lay down to rest.
I walk with the shoestring trailing behind me,
until cat therapist has finished chasing it.
My stiff neck and headache are gone!
It's a cat healing.
I'll be back for more treatments.

Dr. Purrs A. Lot: Exercise improves your ability to concentrate and reduces stress. Canadian Red Cross Blog 2020

CHILLING

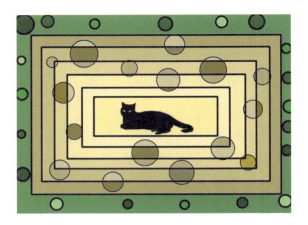

As my cat stares past me, I wonder.
What do you see? I ponder.
Do you see spirits there?
Or bugs floating in the air?
My skin gets a chill as I consider.

Dr. Purrs A. Lot: Do things which add a sense of wonder to your life. Chase flies and chirp at birds. Now everyone is wondering... and you're helping others by making them laugh.

Black Luck

My black cats have brought me a lot of good luck.
Without them, I'd be stuck in the muck.
Much happiness they bring.
My fears? No such thing!
Like an oyster is shucked to find the pearl in the guck.

Dr. Purrs A. Lot: More happiness brings more motivation, which creates more good luck! Rub your cat for good luck.

Queen of Cats

The Queen of Cats was hunting,
for her favourite game.
She did not care for prawns or pawns,
as they both taste the same.
She spent the knight carousing.
First here and then she's there.
She even burned a rookery,
singed feathers filled the air.
"This is just a set piece!"
An arch bishop dared to sing.
So a Chesire grin she gave him,
as she ran off with his King.
(Ben Mikkelsen)

Spend time engaging in games or other hobbies that you enjoy. They give you a break from stress and are good brain exercise.

SAWS

What a little pile of fuzziness,
my tiny kitten of cuteness.
But my! Your claws!
Are they little saws?
As you pounce on my arm with playfulness.

Dr. Purrs A. Lot: Allow more time for play in your life. Start with your kitty.

Roll Out the Mat!

Sometimes my cat gets the zoomies.
He runs to visit his homies.
When he gets there,
no tuna for fare!
He helps out his hungry old cronies.

He caught a fat rat like that!
He thought they should roll out the mat.
"Come, let's not quibble,
but we prefer our kibble."
They said, as he headed back home for pats.

Dr. Purrs A. Lot: Help others freely. Let go of the outcome. As a wise old cat once said, "Raise your tail high and show them what a star you really are".

Cat Plant

Is this a cat plant that I bought?
If I water it, I think that it ought,
to grow kittens for me,
who would sit on my knee.
I'd love to be caught in a kitten onslaught!

Dr. Purrs A. Lot: Surround yourself with pets and people that love you. Caution, you may find yourself buried in love and cat fur.

Cat Acupuncturist

Have you ever considered
cat as acupuncturist?
My cat decides what points I need.
He knows his client well.
His claws activate those points,
and makes me feel just swell?

Dr. Purrs A. Lot: According to Web MD, the article What to Know About Acupuncture for Depression, indicates it can be an effective alternative for some people.

Saviour

Kitty loves to play on the vacuum hose.
When will I get to vacuum? Who knows?
Thank you for saving me.
Now I am free!
To sit on the couch and paint my toes.

Dr. Purrs A. Lot: Treat you and your cat to a spa day! Pick your favourite colour and paint your claws just for fun.

FASHIONISTA

My cat, she jumped into the dryer.
I worried that the heat would fry her!
But Fluffy the cat,
emerged more than that!
She preened and held her head higher!

Dr. Purrs A. Lot: A new hairstyle can improve self-image. Wow your loved ones and strangers alike with a daring cat perm this season! Dare to be that rare, expensive, curly haired cat known
as LaPerm.

Hold It!

My little ball of fuzz sat on my lap.
It was cozy and comfy, that little nap,
Then I had to pee.
Not a choice, you see.
I held on, and restrained the tap!

Dr. Purrs A. Lot: Naps with your cat are refreshing,
Be potty smart and invest in Depends when cat cuddles are on the agenda.

LOVE OR JEALOUSY

Illustration by Ragna Watt

My two cats are staring at me.
Is it with love or jealously?
I was reading a book.
That's all that it took,
for them to ask for attention from me.

Dr. Purrs A. Lot: Everybody knows cats are known for their love of a good book. Read to your cats.

Gone!

My Java with the vibrating tail.
I'm home from work, his tail declares, hail!
Gone for so long,
now that is just wrong!
His meow proclaims with a wail.

Dr. Purrs A. Lot: Make up for lost precious cuddle time while you were at work. Create a healthy balance between work and time spent with loved ones; ESPECIALLY your cat!

Cat's Magic

My cat likes to indulge in cat nip.
He takes a snip and oh what a trip!
He's the craziest I've seen.
He's such a little bean.
Cat's Magic is a better name for that nip!

Dr. Purrs A. Lot: Have fun, get crazy. Be responsible or your cat will scratch you!

Alone Time

My cat has disappeared for a while.
They wanted to be alone, but for me, it's a trial.
I love my special cat.
With them, I love to chat.
When they wake up, I can't help but smile.

Dr. Purrs A. Lot: Cats provide a source of nonjudgmental companionship (despite what the jokes say) not even when they find you sitting on the kitchen floor indulging in a little (or a lot) of midnight ice cream. Not a lick of judgment there, but they might want you to share.

Cat Training

My cat is training me very well.
Turns out, I believe what he tells.
He meows from the stairs
then I have fewer cares.
"Come play with me!" my kitty cat yells.

Dr. Purrs A. Lot: Never underestimate time spent playing with your cat. It will get those wellness chemicals in your body, doPURRmine, oxytocin and serotonin working to keep you and your cat healthy and bonded.

SOFT PREDATOR

BM 2022

Your eyes, they glow so acutely.
In the dark, you hide so astutely.
A soft predator,
hiding in the parlour,
pouncing on my legs so adorably.

Dr. Purrs A. Lot: Make friends with your shadow side and bring it into the light. Just like a black cat is dark and soft, embrace your darkness and soften it. One way is through spiritual beliefs and practices of your choice.

Hat Chase

There once was a cat named Mat,
who felt spiffy in his red cat hat.
The wind blew it off,
but Mat was no sloth,
pouncing after it, he caught that cap!

Dr. Purrs A. Lot: Find what motivates you to exercise. So keep chasing that hat up the stairs, down the stairs, try growing hats in your garden, and picking up those hats around your house. You're bound to be successful!

Secret Keeper

My cat sniffs me to see where I've been.
There's no way I can keep secrets from him.
His nose always knows,
yet, he does not disclose,
but accepts it and tucks under my chin.

Dr. Purrs A. Lot: Find your colony of people and your clowder of felines who accept you.
*Clowder: A group of (cool) cats.

SACRIFICE

My cat loves to scratch on the carpet.
I would rather that she play the trumpet!
Though my carpet has snags,
It looks like a rag!
I'd rather have my cat than a new carpet.

Dr. Purrs A. Lot: 73% of pet owners said their pet enhances their mental health. And 100% of cats couldn't care less, they just want to be loved.
https://www.psychologytoday.com

FELINE FLING

My cat is a wild little thing.
She stares out the window and starts to sing.

In the middle of the night,
I thought that she might,
be telling her boyfriends to come have a fling!

Dr. Purrs A. Lot: Sexual activity can boost your mood and feelings of bonding with your partner. When you feel in heat, don't retreat. Make sure you have consent and both you and your partner's needs and values are respected.

https://www.webmd.com/depression/features/depression-and-sex

Cat Friendship

My cats and I hang out all the time.
We are best of friends, is that such a crime?
I scratch your back,
hey, why did you attack?!
Well, what's a love bite along with some slime.

Dr. Purrs A. Lot: All creatures in your life express their love for you differently. Accept it, but don't let them cross your boundaries. Don't be afraid to hiss when necessary.

Ear Gears

I have a cat with two ears,
that swivel and turn as if on gears.
One to the left.
One to the right.
That cat's ears have periscope mirrors!

Dr. Purrs A. Lot: Enjoy the sounds in your environment, such as the song of the birds, the sound of the leaves crunching beneath your feet or the squeak of the mice in the walls...(!?) or the shaking of your favourite treats rattling in their baggy.

Nine Lives

They say a cat has nine lives.
They juggle knives and chase bees from hives!
Then take a nap,
on top of the lamp.
Climbing up the wall," What a hero!" they cry.

Dr. Purrs A. Lot: Step out of your comfort zone and onto the cat walk. Learn interesting new skills. That how you'll become more resilient.

Fishy

My cat wishes to catch all the fishes.
In the fish tank, my cat squishes,
all the fish with her claws,
there are a few flaws.
When, against her wishes, she swims with those fishes!

 Dr. Purrs A. Lot: Eat fatty fish, take fish oil or algae oil three times per week. Harvard Heath recommended.

GROWING UP

I love you very much, you know.
Got you as a kitten and watched you grow,
from a cute little terror,
now look in the mirror!
"What a beautiful, glowing cat!" I crow.

Dr. Purrs A. Lot: When you look at your cat, intentionally feel the love in your heart and try to keep it there for as long as you can. Click on the link to watch John Kabatt-Zinn Heartscape Meditation
https://www.youtube.com/watch?v=0H20wUUo2-c

Cat Yoga

Where did my cat disappear to?
Did he go to the loo? I don't have a clue.
Maybe he went,
to practice yoga for Lent.
Cats are great at bending in two!

Dr. Purrs A. Lot: Try Yoga to reduce depression and anxiety. Harvard Medical School approved.

CREATIVE PLAY

"Play with me!", my feline friend let on.
She bunted, "Let's get our sillies on!"
But she did not play,
with a string that day.
She found on the ground a round tampon!

She could play with that tampon all day.
Zooming, chasing, jumping, what could I say?
She was having so much fun.
My giggles were unbroken!
I added it to the toys and said, "ooookay".

 Dr. Purrs A. Lot: Put all your paws on the ground and see the world from your cat's point of view. You will gain a new perspective looking at life from different angles. Find ways to harness your imagination and use it to help instead of terrify yourself. See Accelerated Resolution Therapy in the resource section at the end of this book.

Walking Beans

What kind of beans can walk?
Cat paw beans!
What kind of sandpaper is the best quality?
Cat tongues!
What kind of needles are the cutest?
Kitten teeth!
Who makes the best biscuits?
My cat.

Dr. Purrs A. Lot: Allow yourself to be silly. Make the most of your nine lives!

Amusement Park?

Fluffy the cat jumped into the dryer.
It spun and she flew out like a geyser!
So Fluffy the cat,
learned better than that.
The dryer is not a ride, which surprised her!

Dr. Purrs A. Lot: Learn from mistakes instead of beating yourself up. Don't be afraid to climb that tree, you might get stuck but, you can learn new skills to climb back down.

Christmas Glitter

I hear something, is that a bell?
Something, I suspect, is pell-mell.
Their star in the litter,
out poops some glitter,
that they ate when the Christmas tree fell!

Dr. Purrs A. Lot: Look for the humour in life. Laughter helps us cope with unfortunate situations.

Cat Love

Cat Love is the cutest kind of love.
It's pureness and light, like the flight of a dove.
Wait, is that a bird!?
My cat jumped once she heard,
the coo of that dove, and she gave me a shove!

Dr. Purrs A. Lot: No one is purrrrrrfect. Accept each other's flaws with grace.

Sommelier Cat

OLYA VESPYANSKY

My sommelier cat sniffs my plants and vine.
Like fine wine, she wants to taste the divine.
With a sniff, swirl and nip,
she takes a tiny snip.
Only cat nip gives her a good time.

Dr. Purrs A. Lot: Sometimes it takes trying more than one medication to treat a mental illness. It helps to learn new thinking skills or relaxation skills so you can work with the medication.

Cat Scam

There once was a cat named Sam,
who knew she could pull a scam.
She crawled into her bed,
asked for treats to be fed.
"Yes Ma'am!" you adorable little ham.

Dr. Purrs A. Lot: Find out what your core relationship needs are with yourself and others. Then ask for them, and reciprocate. Do you need back scratches, or some biscuits or for someone to clean your litter box? Purrrruse Gary Chap-man's book The 5 Love Languages to learn more about yourself and your partner.

Cat Fever

Meowing frantically, "Don't go to work today".
Shall I call my manager and plaintively say,
"I have come down with cat fever".
Is my manager a believer?
I stay home and wallow in my cats for a day (a mental health day).

Dr. Purrs A. Lot: Pencil in an appointment with your own Dr. Purrs A. Lot.

Be mindful of the signs and symptoms of Cat Fever: uncharacteristic nocturnal liveliness, aversion to all food except for tuna and salmon, uncontrollable urge to pet your cat and the new propensity to swat things off the counter.

Cat Cure

Cats are a cure for loneliness.
In their presence, I feel a holiness.
With a pat of their paw,
I don't feel as raw.
Cats are a cure for anxiousness.

Dr. Purrs A. Lot: As a cat myself, I recommend using a cat as a therapy animal. We love to sit by you, cuddle and bunt you. We love our humans, but show it in different ways. We can sense negative emotions, and we have exceptional communication skills. (usserviceanimals.org)

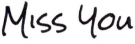

Your eyes and ears are alert while I'm packing.
You hover uneasily and are tracking.
Jumping in and loafing down,
You gently play with my gown.
Do you want to come?
Will you miss your Mom?

Dr. Purrs A. Lot: Losses are a normal part of life. I recommend doing the cat loaf meditation daily.

Mice Dreams

All night long with tail-a-
lashing, deadly paws and stealthy slouch.
You hunted for the sound of scratching, timid twitches,
hungry mouths.
Night has passed and you are
crashing, nose to tail, upon the couch.
40 winks is all you're catching.
Nemesis of bird and mouse.
(Written by Ben Mikkelsen)

Dr. Purrs A. Lot: During emotional situations, or when going through medication changes, it's common to have vivid dreams.

Diva

There once was a cat named Pearly,
whose coat glowed and gleamed very prettily.
They pruned and they preened.
They purred and they screamed,
"I am the prettiest cat in the galaxy!"

Dr. Purrs A. Lot: Positive affirmations work best when you believe them. Cat call yourself until you believe it! https://positivepsychology.com/daily-affirmations/

Black Pearls

My cats are my beautiful black pearls.
Black coats luminescent, light on them swirls.
At just the right angles,
you would think they are angels.
Letting in the light, my wings unfurl.

Dr. Purrs A. Lot: Look for the blessings in unexpected places and difficult circumstances. It will build your resilience.

0200-0530

Asleep in my bed, buried deeply.
Tucked in, snuggled down so sweetly.
Tap, tap, nibble, nibble,
lick, lick, I feel spittle!
My cat wakes me up too early!

Dr. Purrs A. Lot: Make getting enough sleep purrr night a priority for the best mental health.

Cat Help

Every day, you remind me how important you are.
In the fuzziest ways, you tell me, "I'm your star!"
By jumping on my lap,
you help me take a nap.
Your purring sticks me to the couch like tar!

Dr. Purrs A. Lot: Cats purr between 25 and 150 hertz, which are healing frequencies. Cat owners have a 40% less risk of having a heart attack and have lower blood pressure. (This Week Orthopedics, ryortho.com)

Sous Chef

Kitty is my little sous chef.
Stealing my things, she sits on my knife!
"Do not sit there," I say with an air.
I will not eat Potatoes Au Cat Hair!"
She sits there, gives a sniff, and pretends she is deaf.

Dr. Purrs A. Lot: Eating lots of veggies, fruits, fish, lean meats, and whole grains leads to a strong body and a clearer mind. If you eat too much sugar, drink too much alcohol or eat cat hair, expect to feel fuzzy headed.

Night Watch

You guard me nightly
lying by my bedroom door
ready to defend.
Is this your instinct?
Do you love me that much?
My cat, I feel safe.

Dr. Purrs A. Lot: Create a sleep routine that relaxes you and helps you feel safe. Make yourself your favourite tea (chamomile or cat nip works wonders), find your coziest nook, curl up in a ball and purr the night away.

TROUBLE!

There once was a cat named Noodle,
who loved to lick the strudel.
Her paws got stuck.
Such bad luck!
She was stuck in a puddle of trouble.

Dr. Purrs A. Lot: When you get into the same kind of trouble repeatedly, look at what rewards you are getting from it. How can you get those rewards in a healthier way?

Bathtub Pub

Mr Cat jumps into the bathtub.
"Kind sir," I say, "Welcome to the pub.
In Winter, Nordic water,
in Spring, fresh spring water".
"Nordic water please" in the bathtub pub.

Dr. Purrs A. Lot: Staying hydrated will contribute to better attention and focus. Drink that glass of water you left lying around before your cat does!

Live Mouse!

How do I know that you love me?
It's in the gifts that you bring me, you see.
One day you went out.
That day I leapt about!
A mouse dropped out of your mouth and went squee!

Dr. Purrs A. Lot: It's worth finding out what your partner's and friend's love languages are to make sure those are squeals of delight and not horror.

Rad Cats

There once were two cats with a Dad,
who scritched and they scratched and were bad!
"More treats!", they did yell,
tripping Dad straight to hell!
Dad was not mad, us cats are so rad!

Dr. Purrs A. Lot: Cats are rad, no scholarly reference needed.

Simply Heartfelt

The bond between my cat and I
is a primal kind of love.
It quiets my thoughts and
head's simply straight to my heart.

Dr. Purrs A. Lot: Loving Kindness Cat Meditation: Put your paw on your heart and think about your cat. Focus on the fuzzy feeling in times of stress.

Play Time

There once was a cat with a toy,
who jumped, and ran and cried, "oy!"
"What fun!" they meowed.
Oh my, they were loud!
Then that poor toy they destroyed.

Dr. Purrs A. Lot: Physical play reduces your levels of stress hormones cortisol and adrenalin and triggers the release of wellness hormones to increase your mood. Laughter increases those feel good hormones, so laugh with your cat as they play.
(nbcnews.com)

Insomnia

There once was a cat named Willy,
who thought his Dad's head was always chilly.
He licked Dad's hair,
dad was caught in his lair!
Dad couldn't sleep, but he loved that Willy.

Dr. Purrs A. Lot: You may have to set boundaries with loved ones to improve your mental health. Let others know where your territory is by spraying... with lavender, mostly.....

Persistence

There once was a cat named Noodle
who loved to huddle and cuddle.
She fell off my lap,
went tumble and flap,
felt in a muddle, but came back for more cuddles!

Dr. Purrs A. Lot: Think of something you're good at to build your confidence. Your cat already thinks you're purrrrfect.

Tutor

My cat was pawing the computer,
composing a piece of literature.
"Hey tiddle, diddle,
the cat had a fiddle."
And now they shall need a tutor.

Dr. Purrs A. Lot: Don't be afraid to ask for a paw when in knead.

What gift did you bring me, my little predator.
Is it a bird or a mouse turnover?
Perhaps it's a vole,
or maybe a mole?
You are the cutest, the softest little murderer.

Dr. Purrs A. Lot: Kind and generous acts such as giving gifts to others increases levels of happiness and well-being. (American Psychological Association. apa.org) Accept your cat's gifts and pay it forward.

DAD'S GONE

There once was a cat name Kyla.
When her Dad took a trip, she signed a
deal with her Mom,
to always stay calm
and ran herself down to the spa.

Dr. Purrs A. Lot: Take some time from your busy schedule to treat yourself to a grooming session.

Spooky Chair

My black chair has a pair of yellow eyes.
I should bring it to market and claim a prize!
For that black chair,
also grew hair!
Or was it my shadowy black cat in disguise?

Dr. Purrs A. Lot: When we are struggling with mental health, all we see are monsters. Learn the skill of naming the monster to rid it of it's power. Click the link to learn more https://positivepsychology.com/emotion-regula-tion/

Soft Claws

Your fur is so soft and luxurious.
When you knead on my lap, it's glorious.
Though your claws dig in,
I don't make a din,
because for that you are notorious.

Dr. Purrs A. Lot : Life is both pleasure and pain. Acknowledge the discomfort, but focus on the pawsitive.

Shadows

Two black cats follow me around.
My shadows,
they don't make a sound.
Bad luck? I think not!
Until I am caught.
My shadows
trip me in one bound!

Dr. Purrs A. Lot: Life will trip you up sometimes, but keep putting one paw in front of the other. It's ok to crawl. You **will** learn to walk again.

Tight Rope Walker

My cat thinks she can walk a tight rope.
She is very optimistic, she has a lot of hope.
She sees the cupboard edge,
tries to walk on that ledge!
Falls flat on her butt, but she can cope.

Dr. Purrs A. Lot: Life can feel like walking a tight rope. A wrong sidestep could end in a fall. Are all falls bad? Is there a lesson in it? You decide.

Be Furbulous

There once was a gorgeous black cat,
who knew he was fab and all that!
When the lights went out,
"Turn them on!" he would shout.
He disappeared in the dark, that poor cat.

Dr. Purrs A. Lot: Embrace your strengths and shine your light on the world. Be your furbulous self!

Dish Duty

There once was a cat named Bob,
who decided he should have a job.
He licked all the dishes,
from the counter he wishes,
that the plates had not fallen, sobbed Bob.

Dr. Purrs A. Lot: It's ok to cry over sp lled milk. Expressing your feelings helps you get through them.

Fussy Cat

There once was a very fussy cat,
who said, "Play with me, but not like that!
" You must guess what I'll play,
every other day!"
And with that, they lay flat on the mat!

Dr. Purrs A. Lot: Purrrrsistence is key to achieving your goals.

A Break in my Clouds

When the world is too loud,
I want to cuddle in a shroud.
I turn to my cat,
"What do you think about that?"
My cat turns to me,
"What will happen to me?"
I get a raspy kiss and cuddle.
Kitty and I cocoon and huddle.
Maybe I don't need a shroud.
There is finally a break in my clouds.

 Dr. Purrs A. Lot: When you feel like you're going to drown in your dark cloud, tell a loved one or call a suicide distress line. Dedicated to all whose cats have saved their lives.

Cat Rescue

Drip, drip went the bathtub faucet.
I could hear it from my downstairs closet!
"I can help with that,"
said my very own cat.
He drank all the drips before I lost it!

Dr. Purrs A. Lot: You don't have to cope alone. Ask for help, then accept it when it arrives.

Feline Fantasy

There once was a cat named Mai Tai,
who wanted to lick the sky.
When her brother was near,
she said, "Hey, come here!"
He lifted her high and she tasted the sky!

Dr. Purrs A. Lot: Spend time around people and cats who lift your spirits.

INVASION

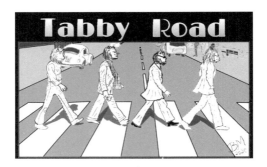

There once was a cat named Fantasia,
who played with my wool straight from Asia.
She jumped on my lap,
as I was knitting a cap.
It was plainly a kitty cat invasion!

Dr. Purrs A. Lot: Pick up a hobby that both you and your cat can enjoy. Yarn is fun to knit and chase!

Cat Healing

My cats healed my back pain.
My cats healed my broken heart ... a few times.
My cats quieted my restless mind.
My cats taught my family how to love each other better.

Dr. Purrs A. Lot: Follow your cat's teachings. Even when you experience set backs in your mental wellness goals, keep practicing those mental wellness skills until they become a new habit. Your cat is there for you and so are we.

COMFORT

I was hurried, I was worried, I was stressed.
Fumbling with my clothes to get dressed.
My cats were nearby,
and they saw me cry.
Head boop, cuddle, kiss, I am blessed.

Dr. Purrs A. Lot: Be like the cat, slow down, unwind that fur ball in your brain by paying attention to your surroundings, ie your cat.

Cat Night Nurse

0200 pat, pat, lick, nibble, cuddle.
0400 pat, pat, lick, nibble, cuddle.
It's the cat night nurse mandate
To check on beloved human,
Every two hours (q2h),
all night long.
Comfort Rounds

Dr. Purrs A. Lot: I know you love your cat, but if they are keeping you awake, you have my blessing to close your bedroom door.

Fishbowl Margarita

My cat loves their fishbowl margarita.
As they drink it, they decide to treat a
fish with a kiss.
Oh, what bliss!
That fish is such a dish! Deliciosa!

Dr. Purrs A. Lot: Eating fish is always a choice on a date. Find out what your fish likes and have fun.

Feline Frolicking

The five rights of feline frolicking:
Your feline must be in the right mood,
you must choose the right toy and play the right game,
in the right environment with the right person.
Other than that, be carefree and enjoy frolicking with your feline.

Dr. Purrs A. Lot: Be like the cat and get to know your own preferences in life and honour them.

Human Friend

I like to wind myself around your soft head
and groom you while you lay in bed.
I know I'll have to move,
but right now I'll soothe,
my warm, stressed human friend.

Dr.Purrs A. Lot: See yourself through the eyes of your cat and love yourself more.

Cozy Time

You like to nibble and lick my nose.
You especially like to attack my toes!
But when we cuddle,
you are such a puddle.
As I huddle down with my kitty when it snows.

Dr. Purrs A. Lot: This technique is called Kitty Cat Cuddle Meditation. Practice daily.

CHRISTMAS ELF

I think my cat is a Christmas Elf.
They love wrapping paper and ribbon, and like to sit on the shelf.

They even have claws. Are they related to Claus? They sit under the tree, and dance with Santa Claus.

Dr. Purrs A. Lot: During the busyness of Christmas, remember to be still for a few moments to soak up the Christmas spirit.

Cat Nip

Here you are, "I love you dear,"
my cat purrs in my ear.
Grooming me lazily
I relax so easily...
Then, a little NIP!
Wrong kind of cat nip...

Dr. Purrs A. Lot: Your cat will help you stay mentally alert...even when you don't want to.

CHAMPAGNE BUBBLES

Cats are like the champagne bubbles in life,
making me giggle in times of strife.
They reach up and tickle my nose,
and sometimes spill across my toes.
Some are fast and sparkling, some are slow and gassy,
Every one of them reminds me to stay classy,
and a little sassy.

Dr. Purrs A. Lot: Respect yourself, no matter what side of your personality is showing that day. Love yourself when you're sparkling and when you're gassy.

Cat Croissant

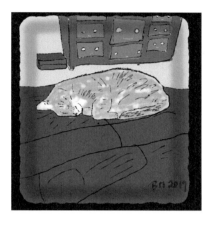

Can we replace the expression "curled up in the fetal position"
with "curled up in the cat croissant position?"
At least this has a cute elegance to it,
instead of feeling like a baby when we're feeling low.
Let's respect ourselves even in our lowest times.

Dr. Purrs A. Lot: Listen to your cat's purr and let it comfort you when you are upset. Show yourself compassion. To learn self compassion, follow this link
https://self-compassion.org/category/exercises/

Black Crystal

I hope to see triple this New Year's Eve.
No, not drinking a cocktail or two or three.
I have one eye in the past,
one eye in the present,
and one eye in the future.
All at once, I am in all times,
with my cat on my lap to ground me,
they are a black crystal,
that refracts my life's light,
and shows me all my colours are beautiful.

Dr. Purrs A. Lot: Reflect on your past and present strengths. What strengths do you want to build in the future?

MAJOR TOM

As he climbed up on the gantry,
he remembered climbing Gran's tree.
She was always where he would like to be.
They would talk and they would groom,

as they looked up at the moon,
These hunters softly wondered,
if cats would walk there soon.

So he did train and he did study.
How do you always land on your feet?
When you're afloat on a space boat, falling weightlessly.

Orbits and reaction mass,
He studied hard and studied fast.
His brow would furrow and his tail would lash. As he fought to excel and then fought to surpass.

Now he's arrived at the Very Big Day.
Leading the crew that will soon blast away.
His fear made him stop and have a quick pray. For the pride of his Pride, will he die on this day?

It was hard to climb on,
and show some aplomb.
These rockets, after all, are just flying bombs!
Keep a stiff upper muzzle and keep the crew calm.
Who are you, after all?
You're Major Tom!

If his Gran could see him now,
she'd prob'ly sniff, "meow".
No need to bluff, I know it's tough, you'll pull through
if you have the Right Fluff.

It could have been a catastrophe.
Instead, they entered history.
With one ginger step for kitty,
he made a leap for lunar seas.
(by Ben Mikkelsen)

Dr. Purrs A. Lot : Learn to encourage yourself. You can achieve your dreams.

https://positivepsychology.com/daily-affirmations/

Online Mental Health Resources

- Canadian Mental Health Association has two free online courses you can take called Mental Health Awareness and Stress Management And Healthy Coping.

- Canadian Red Cross has psychological first aid courses to help you build resilience when you have experienced stress, crisis or trauma. The cost is $20 Canadian each and are called Self-Care, and Caring for Others.

- John Kabatt-Zinn YouTube video series explaining Mindfulness and how to practice meditation.

- For a list of positive affirmations, this article has separate lists for men and women. Ignore the categories and choose the affirmations that resonate with you.

- Accelerated Resolution Therapy developed by Laney Rosenzweig MS, LMFT is an innovative approach to trauma therapy using your imagination and eye movements. Videos are available online describing this therapy in detail. There are therapists who practice this in the US and Canada, search your province or state for practitioners.

- Gary Chapman has an online course called The 5 Love Languages for $20.00.

- See this Positive Psychology site to learn more about naming emotions

- Dr. Kristen Kneff, Psychologist, studies self-compassion.

- ADHD 2.0: New Science and Essential Strategies for Thriving with Distraction from Childhood to Adulthood.

- The Autism Discussion Page on Stress, Anxiety, Shutdowns and Meltdowns by Bill Nason.

- Hypnotherapy can be very helpful for some people. I used self hypnosis at a time when I needed to relearn how to relax. The relaxation was profound. I used the website Uncommon Knowledge, which is a UK company run by two Psychologists. Their prices are reasonable and they offer a lot of free information.

- See this short Jaxon Galaxy video on Pet Therapy.

Manufactured by Amazon.ca
Bolton, ON